PATHWAY TO SUCCESS

,,

Definitive principles for achievement

ADEOLA BABATUNDE

The names and identifying characteristics of certain individuals referenced in this publication have been changed. This publication contains the opinions and ideas of its author.

For more information, send your mail to:info@adeolababatunde.com

---

Printed in the United States of America

© Adeola Babatunde 2014

www.adeolababatunde.com

Published by: David Daniel consultancy Ltd

ISBN- 978-1-326-01379-0

Acknowledgement

Special thanks to my wife (Bola) and Children (David, Daniel and Debbie) who gave me the time and space to write.

To my brothers and Sisters who have always been there for me.

To the authors and teachers I have learnt from, for their guidance and support along the way

To my clients who allowed me to share what I have learnt through relating with them.

You may have picked this book solely for the purpose of learning some quick tips on how to discover the potential in you, if that is the case, I am sure you will find many useful ideas that will help you work on your potential. It is my hope that you will become interested in going further and embrace some of these ideas as part of a longer-range, deeper, and broader change process leading to greater self-discovery and personal growth. I also hope that you will be able to use this greater self-understanding and personal development to make conscious choices that will help you to grow and evolve your unique potential in life.

Happy Reading.

Contents

1

Success and Power

The mind plays an important role in achieving every kind of success and goal, minor, everyday goals or major goals. With minor or day-to-day goals, one usually knows what he or she wants to do or get, but when it comes to major goals, most people don't know what they really desire. They desire to do something big, but they don't know what. They might have a vague idea, but this is not enough. To accomplish anything, and to use your mind power, you have to know exactly what it is you want to do. To focus your mind power on a goal, you need to have a clear and well defined goal. How do you go about that? You have first to think or meditate, to find out what is it that you want to accomplish or gain. This might not be a simple step, and requires deep thinking, investigation and time.

After discovering what you really want to accomplish, you need to come up with a plan for action. You need to know what you have to do first and how to proceed. All of this requires planning, which means using the power of the mind.

After deciding on a goal and coming up with a plan, you need to hold in your mind a clear mental image of your goal. You need to see it accomplished. This step requires that you use your imagination, which is another power of the mind. Not everyone can visualise clear mental images, but regular training of the imagination can do wonders. You may, for example, look at photos of what you want to achieve, and then close your eyes, and try to see it in your imagination. This will enhance your ability to visualise. At this point you have to display patience, self-discipline and the power to persist in your efforts. This requires a one pointed mind.

Affirmations are another useful mental tool for achieving success. What you affirm sinks into the subconscious mind, becomes part of the subconscious mind, and consequently affects your behaviour and actions. If your affirmations are positive, they lead you to success. Another important power of the mind is thought transference. You need to be able to transmit your thoughts to other people, who would aid you with your plans. Often, you have to persuade others to invest in your plans or to help you in other ways. It is not enough just to talk with them, you need to believe in what you are saying; you need to be enthusiastic and persuasive, otherwise they won't listen and won't care. You need to be able to reject doubts. To be able to do so, you need concentration, control over your thoughts, willpower, self-discipline and patience. All these are mental tools and skills.

Motivation is another mental and emotional power that you require for achieving success. How can you achieve anything if you are not motivated enough? To increase your motivation and enthusiasm, think often of your goal, about its advantages and benefits, and how it will change your life. Doing so, will strengthen you. Your thoughts, which are part of your mind, possess power. The thoughts that you most often think tend to come true. If you pour your mental energy into the same thoughts or mental images day after day, they will become stronger and stronger, and would consequently affect your attitude, expectations, behaviour and actions. These thoughts and mental images can even be subconsciously perceived by other people, who would then offer you help or opportunities. Your thoughts can also create what is usually termed as coincidence. They can attract into your life corresponding events, situations and opportunities.

Not every thought turns into reality. A thought has to be repeated often, and be tinged with desire, in order to come true. Doubts, fears and worries tend to destroy what you build with the power of your mind. This means that you need to clear your mind of negative thoughts and doubts. You might say that this is not possible, but it is, through proper training, articles, e-books and books. Did you ever stop and wonder what life would be like if Wilbur and Orville Wright hadn't given us the airplane? What about Thomas Edison and the light bulb?

Helen Keller was deaf and blind before the age of two. Yet she accomplished great works that have benefited others tremendously and still impacts people's lives today. Imagine, what if these great achievers had not dreamt their dreams? Did they possess a secret formula for success or were they just that much smarter than everyone else?

Clearly life was not easy street for any of those mentioned here. Maybe they and other of our modern day heroes are just born with certain gifts and abilities that you and I are not. I don't know for sure but I don't think these extraordinary people necessarily had extraordinary talent. Maybe they just had an extraordinary belief in themselves. Maybe, just maybe they knew the four words that create power and guarantee success, and they used those words to accomplish what they did. Ponderous isn't it?

I believe that they did know those four words. I believe they used those words every single day of their life and by doing so they became great achievers in our society. Those words were so much a part of their lives that they didn't even have to think about using them. It was a subconscious, natural act for them. Perhaps in the beginning these heroes didn't use the magical words. But soon came to realise their power, soon began to use them habitually, and ultimately they were integrated into their thinking, their dreaming and their speech.

Do you know the four words?

Before I tell you, ask yourself this question. If I had the four words that would give me unstoppable power and guaranteed success would I use them? Power is a responsibility. When you have it you have an advantage so you must be deliberate in its use. Think about where you would use this power of accomplishment. Would it be in managing your weight, or getting fit? Maybe you have another priority; I don't know but think about it. These are really powerful words. They can change your life. They can change how you see things. You will look at problems differently and no longer be afraid. You will notice the miracle of positive coincidence. What are the words?

The four words that will create power and guarantee success are: 'What - Can - I - Do". Uh, that's it? Yes, those are the four words that create unstoppable power. For any given problem or situation you have choices. You can either ask "why does this always happen to me", or you could say, "why does this have to happen now", or you could say, "when will somebody (else) do something about this", or you could say this: "What - Can - I - Do that will turn this situation around?" "What - Can - I - Do that will stop this from happening?" "What " Can - I - Do to take action right now?" "What - Can - I - Do to get me one step closer to my goal?" A variation of those four words and ones that are equally as powerful are: "How - Can - I - ...? Complete the phrase and you'll see what I mean. For example, "How - Can - I - take action now that will change the status quo?" "How can I - do things differently and get a better result?" "How can I - change my behaviour?"

Do you see how different those questions are than the "Why" questions? Nobody has the ability to effect more change over your life than you do. So why would any of us ever ask "When are they going to" or, "when will he/she", or "why can't someone else" or, "why can't this situation be different?" A question with no actionable answer is a circular question. The answers will never really solve a problem or give cause for a true call to action. Alternatively, the "what can I do" questions have just the opposite effect and will give rise to action.

Your life is a reflection of your thoughts, your words and dreams. The quality of the questions you ask will determine the quality of those thoughts and the quality of life that we all will live. Whatever problem you are facing today has an answer. You can get closer to that answer just by asking a better question. An answer may not be evident immediately but you'll get an answer. In fact, you already have the answer you just need to awaken it with one of those powerful, take action questions. You can start asking better questions today and see the miracles unfold. Alternatively, you can ask "why this or why that" and run the risk of never getting off that hamster wheel of frustration.

Today, I challenge you to begin the practice of asking really good questions. I challenge you to unleash the power of your own words, thoughts and dreams.

Have you ever given much "thought" with regard to what your thoughts are, where they come from or the power they have in moulding and shaping your life? Have you ever considered the fact that your thoughts are derived from and triggered as the result of pure consciousness?

If you're like the vast majority, the answer is "No". That's what we'll be looking at here...The Power of Thoughts...more specifically the power of your individual thoughts and the crucial role they play in determining how every event, condition and circumstance in your life unfolds as a result of their creative power. Although it isn't the power of your thoughts alone that determine how things unfold, your chosen thoughts combined with the power of emotions that these chosen thoughts ignite, most certainly do.

Understanding and learning to consciously and intentionally implement the power of your thoughts is a vital and necessary component of achieving and experiencing your most sought after dreams and desires. On a larger scale, it is crucial to human evolution. For some, to fully grasp and understand how and why the Power Of thoughts mould and shape their lives, it may be helpful...necessary even to delve into and discover the role that consciousness plays, not only in your individual life, but in every aspect of creation. When you grasp and begin to really understand how your conscious mind as well as your subconscious mind are infused and interact with Universal Consciousness. You can really begin to get really excited about your individual potential and what is available to you and for you.

You can really begin to appreciate the role that the power of your thoughts plays which at the same time, when you learn to "consciously direct" the emotions that your thoughts ignite begin to both understand and see in a "real and tangible" way what a profound and transformational difference your individual mind power plays in the process.

Developing a crystal clear understanding as to how the power of thoughts affect every area of your life will serve to provide not only the "desired" outcomes experienced in your physical world but prove to provide you with unfailing and timeless wisdom that will provide immense benefit toward enhancing your mental, emotional and spiritual growth, understanding, and provide a sense of peace, wellbeing and overall fulfilment in every aspect of life as well .As you'll soon discover anything and everything in the world begins and happens as a result of the power of thoughts. The predominant thoughts that you choose to think combined with the emotions that these chosen thoughts create will, with unwavering certainty mould and shape your life physically, financially, relationally, emotionally and spiritually.

Thought is quite literally the often overlooked seed that shapes your external world. Our world or the entire cosmos for that matter wouldn't exist if it were not for the fact that God, Gaia, Allah, Source, Universal Intelligence, Higher Consciousness (or whatever you perceive the Source to be) first had a "conceptualisation" and/or a thought to create it. "Sure", you say. "But that was God that did that; I'm just a human Being. You're saying that the power of thoughts can affect my individual circumstances too?" Good question. So let's take a look at the power of thoughts in the "physical realm" and more specifically in your life. Think deeply about this for a minute. Had Alexander Graham Bell not thought that he could invent a device that would allow you to pick up a device with numerous holes in each end, one that you could hear from and talk into, as well as transmit your voice thousands of miles in lightning fast time, you wouldn't have the convenience of, or ability to, pick up the telephone and talk to someone on the other side of the world.

If the Wright Brothers hadn't first conceived the thought that they could create a machine that would allow people to seemingly defy the law of gravity, we wouldn't know what it was like, or be able to, board an airplane with the ability to travel from one side of the country to the other in a matter of a few hours. What about Colonel Sanders? What would the world be like without Kentucky Fried Chicken!!! OK...just kidding, but you get the idea. :)

These are just a few of the infinite number of examples as to how the power of thoughts have transformed and impacted our world. Now, obviously the above examples were not just thought into existence. They are mentioned to express the importance of the power of thoughts or more specifically, the conceptualisation of a particular thought which serves as the seed that initiated the process for these things to be made "real." But, had the seed never been planted, the harvest would not and could not exist. Once the seed is planted, it does have to be nurtured in order to reach full maturity. But the whole process begins at the level of consciousness. It's consciousness that enables a thought to be thought initially. Consciousness is the "spiritual or if you prefer the unseen realm and thought is the first step in the process that makes all this "spiritual stuff" "real and tangible."

Without the power of thought, you have no power. I'm sure there are still some who are thinking to themselves, "Well yea, but these guys who made all these world changing discoveries and inventions had great minds and big educations." Fair enough, let's bring it closer to home where you can see for yourself the impact that the power of thoughts...more specifically "individual thoughts" can have when put into action. Think about the People In your immediate circle of influence...In your Personal Life....

This will begin to give you some deeper insight as to the power of thoughts in your own world and how they affect you individually. Stop and think for a moment about the different people in your life. Your family, friends, colleagues, and people you work with etc.

By listening to what they say, you can come pretty close to determining what their predominant thought patterns are and begin to develop a deeper understanding of how the power of thoughts fit into each individual circumstance. In thinking about each of them individually, do you know anyone that constantly communicates a lack of money? If you do, I'd be willing to base my reputation on the fact that they don't have enough...or at least "perceive" that they don't. I'd be willing to bet that they are always scraping and struggling regardless of how hard they might "work" just to make ends meet. That is the power of thoughts in action. Do you know of anyone that continually talks negatively about a specific relationship that they are in? Again, I can assure you that the relationship that they continually express dissatisfaction with is lacking in some way. That too is the power of thoughts in action. Now think about someone who constantly talks or worries about being ill. You bet, they are ill a great deal of the time. They get the flu every time the flu comes around. They get a cold every time they're exposed to the virus, etc.

Now let's shift gears a bit...

How about someone that you know that is positive and upbeat all the time? In the same respect, their results in life will show it. Their external outcomes (events, conditions and circumstances in life) are a direct reflection of their internal thought processes. There are exceptions for sure. It would be impossible to address all of these exceptions here without changing this book into an Encyclopaedia Britannica, but as a general rule, the same holds true. Each of these outcomes are excellent examples of the power of thoughts in action.

You are probably thinking to yourself, "Well yea, they are thinking these things because that is the situation they are in!" This is where you need to make a major shift in your thinking. A paradigm shift. The reason they are in the situation they are in is because of the predominant thoughts and beliefs of lack (fear) and limitation that they have established, which are exactly what attracted and created the situation in the first place.

Until they are willing and able to change the initial underlying thought process that created the situation, and/or the emotions that accompany these patterns, they will continue to attract and experience the same results, and they will remain "seemingly stuck" in that situation.

Let me repeat...

Until the consistent, self-limiting thought process is changed that created the situation initially, the exact same results will continue. This pattern will continue to repeat itself over and over and over again until the thought process is changed and a different belief is established which will automatically attract the resources or conditions required and needed for a different outcome! The conventional wisdom of the world is, "I'll believe it when I see it." The unwavering and immutable principles known as Universal Laws make certain that unless and until you "Believe it, you will not see it!" The great teacher Jesus said; "Therefore I say unto you, what things so ever ye *desire* when ye pray, believe that ye receive them and ye shall have them.

He doesn't say you'll receive them first so you can believe them! He says believe and you shall receive.

This isn't just evident and based on spiritual writings and teachings, modern day science has also discovered and documented the creative power of thoughts combined with emotions in relation to life and manifesting outcomes in the physical world starting back in 1925! It's the same in your life and the life of everyone else on this planet!! The Power of thoughts play a huge and tremendous role in determining the kind and quality of your life...period. The kind and quality of the consistent thoughts you choose define, mould and shape the kind and quality of your life physically, financially, relationally, emotionally and/or spiritually. The people we discussed who you know are not thinking those thoughts because that is their situation, although that is how the majority believe it works. That is only a perception of truth. An extremely limited perception that will keep them "stuck" in the same cycle. They themselves are creating what they don't want and all the while "thinking and believing" that they have no control over the process. Granted, they may be doing so "unconsciously", yet they are "doing it" just the same. Let's equate the predominant thoughts that we choose to think as "being." Whatever we are choosing to "be" at any given moment without fail determines what we do and as a result determines what we'll have or not have.

The creative process is immutable and unwavering. It never rests. Everyone with the ability to think is quite literally creating something every second of every minute of every day. Without fully understanding the creative process, more specifically, what a crucial role the power of thoughts play in that process, the outcomes experienced in every aspect of your and everyone else's life...although they are and will continue to be "the seed" that determines "the harvest", are in the vast majority of cases being planted "Unconsciously."

The result is that the vast majority "perceive" that the world...more specifically the outcomes experienced in their lives are "random and chaotic" at best. The process is never random and chaotic. It's always harmonious. It's often "perceived" as being "random" only because we choose to engage the power of thoughts "unconsciously."

The simple fact that those mentioned earlier continually think about each of these occurrences is enough to allow the subconscious mind to begin the process of what it is designed to do. It absorbs the "conscious thought" as truth, depending on the emotional response and intensity of the thought it stores it as a memory picture, and begins the process that will actually cause whatever is consistently held as thought to happen in the physical world. When it is reinforced with words, (brought into the physical realm) and the emotions attached to it are elevated, it will actually *speed up the process!*.

I personally know of many people, who I have been introduced to through the years, who by their consistent words and actions, (and obviously unaware of the creative power of thoughts) continually bring about circumstances in their lives that are in complete opposition to what it is they claim that they have a desire to experience. They overlook the simplicity and perfection of the process.

One lady in particular that comes to mind, we'll call her Julie, (an alias) has gone through most of her life declaring how horrible everything is. Although she claimed and truly desired to experience a better quality of life, she chose to remain unaware of the power of thoughts...more specifically her individually chosen and consistently focused on thoughts and as a result allows her "unconscious" thought patterns to dictate and create what is produced in every aspect of her life. Her life unfolds just as she chooses and guess what. It's horrible. She gets to be right. If the temperature outside were above 80 degrees, it was horrible. If the weather delivered temperatures below 45 degrees it was horrible. If there were a few too many cars on the road, the traffic was horrible. It doesn't matter what the situation was, it was horrible. Sadly, I have watched this lady's life be, you guessed it, horrible.

She is by her own choosing creating what she "perceives" as horrible while at the same time feeling as if she is a "victim" of circumstance. But she isn't!! She is an "unconscious creator" of her horrible circumstances. It's simply a matter of "perception" which continues to create these "horrible" circumstances which continues to show up in her life as horrible. As much as I would try to share the knowledge that I've learnt concerning the creative power of thoughts and the emotions this train of thought creates, although she would listen occasionally, she never really absorbed and implemented these truths into her life. As a result, she has always been short of money, unhappy in her relationships, and suffers poor health.

She is about as far away from abundance and happiness as anyone could be. As sad as that is, she has brought it about through her predominant thought process, and reinforced it with her words which are exactly what created the conditions that she claims that she doesn't want to experience.

Although I use this specific example, the power of thoughts are just as creative and precise in producing a harvest for you, me and anyone else who has the ability to think and reason. There is another area where people fail to grasp and fully understand how the power of thoughts "unconsciously" impact their lives. You Can never create what you want by keeping your Predominant focus on what you don't want. I encounter and communicate with a number of people who do understand the power of thoughts yet are "unconsciously" sabotaging the creation of what they "claim" they want. Many times although they may consciously desire a specific outcome, their predominant focus is placed on what they don't have or don't want rather than what it is they desire to experience. The inevitable result, due to the immutable and unwavering creative power of thoughts, and their "unconsciously focused" thoughts, combined with the "fear based" emotions that follow, create more of what they don't desire. As a specific example let's assume someone was consistently "thinking about" "Not" wanting to be broke. Not wanting to be broke can only create more of being broke. Why? Because, it takes thoughts of abundance and prosperity combined with the emotions that these thought create to create abundance and prosperity...not the absence of being broke.

The subconscious mind is non-discerning and doesn't exercise the same "rational" thought process as the "conscious mind" does. It accepts whatever data it's provided. It's non discerning. It doesn't differentiate between "positive and negative." It doesn't conceive and comprehend the "negative." I suppose you could say it innocently accepts and records whatever data it's provided.

2

Create Your Reality

It is possible for someone to be negative regarding a specific relationship and still have a great deal of financial wealth. If you were to dig deeper you would find that, their predominant thoughts regarding their relationship were something less than positive, but their thoughts regarding wealth or money are harmonious with having it and through the unwavering and immutable process of creation which is governed by Universal Laws, that I like to refer to as "The Perfect Plan", it is provided to them.

Likewise, it is also possible to know someone with abundant health, who can't seem to get ahead in the financial arena. You would find the same principle to be true. The predominant mental thought processes regarding health would be positive, but the thought or attitude (seed) toward finances would be lacking providing a harvest that harmonises with the seed.

What is crucial for you to understand is this, If you choose to have an abundant, happy, balanced, and harmonious Life, a kind and quality of life that the vast majority don't, your predominant thoughts need to be focused on and in harmony with what is desired and not what is lacking.

The Universal Laws that govern the process of creation, which by the way have existed since the beginning of time itself, will make certain that what is "asked" for, is precisely what is received. When you establish and choose to hold a belief that something will happen, regardless if it is in the physical, financial, relational, emotional and/or spiritual aspect of your life, the vibrational frequency and intensity of the power of thoughts, more specifically the emotions which these thoughts create and ignite, will harmonise with and attract precisely that which is thought and believed. You simply cannot escape the immutable, unwavering and perfect process of creation. Now let's dig a little deeper and discover a little more about how the power of thoughts combined with Universal Laws create our reality.

How does your thought affect your experience In Life?

OK...now that we have the "big picture view" of the power of thoughts let's cover the "process" of how all these things that we choose to "think" are made "real and tangible due to the power of thoughts. Understanding and consciously directing the power of thoughts is what will shape *your* world in a way that you desire. Thoughts are a living, vibrating mass of energy packets (photons) that are every bit as real and alive as you and I. They cannot be sensed or experienced with the five basic human senses of hearing, sight, smell, touch, or taste. But they are certainly real, and will ultimately determine your success (or the lack of) in life.

Your whole existence, everything that is, and everything that you experience in your day to day life is brought about solely on what has recently been labelled "The Law of attraction" . It is also known as other names such as," Sowing and Reaping", (in the Christian community) Karma, (Buddhist) or as science refers to it, Cause and Effect. What you choose to call it is immaterial. All are one and the same and act in exact accordance with how the Universe was created to operate. There are a number of people in the world today that would nitpick and argue about which of these labels is correct. What they would find if they chose to delve deeper, keep an open mind, eliminate judgmental type thinking, and investigate the reasoning and deeper meaning behind each, is that they are all one and the same, and each of them are absolutely correct!

Our current and ancestral Spiritual Teachers as well as the many great Spiritual writings available to us, clearly tell us that whatever it is we sow (or do) we will reap (receive) accordingly. What does that have to do with the power of thoughts? The thought is literally "the seed" that you are sowing and emotion is the fertilizer that feeds and nourishes the originally conceived thought seed.

In Buddhist teachings, the Law of Karma, says this: "*For every event that* occurs, *(initial act) there will follow another event whose existence was* caused *by the first, and that, this second event (the outcome) will be pleasant or unpleasant based on the skilfulness of (or the unskillfulness of) the act which caused it.*

What does this have to do with the power of thoughts? The thought acts as the cause of the event. Nothing can happen unless a thought is first conceived. Science states that *"For every cause (action) there must be an equal effect"*.(outcome) Again the thought acts as the "Cause." The only difference in the three is in the presentation or delivery, and the perception of the hearer. While many have heard these various truths, the majority only relate them to visible physical activity and fail to look deeply enough to develop the understanding that in order for a physical activity to happen, it must first begin as a thought or consciousness. (the cause) When you begin to "truly" grasp this you begin to clearly see and understand the creative power of thought and how it can and does impact every aspect of your life.

As mentioned earlier anything and everything which has been created, is being created or ever will be created is the result of consciousness, a process which begins as an unseen, meta-physical or spiritual event which is stirred and the process of creation is initiated by the power of thoughts.

The bottom line is, your thoughts are the initial unseen seed that determine the outcomes that you will experience in the physical world. Just as you plant a seed in the soil, it must surely produce a plant of like proportion to the seed that was planted. If you were to plant crabgrass seeds you certainly couldn't expect them to produce a big beautiful Oak tree. If you plant crabgrass seeds you get crabgrass. If you plant an apple seed you receive an apple tree.

This simple Universal Principle is known to all. Even a young child understands this.

With that being "true", why would it be any different with our thoughts? It isn't! That is great news! Why? Because by developing an understanding of this simple principle, by becoming "conscious" of the consistent thoughts that we choose to think, we can then go to work on restructuring and Implementing the power of thoughts, (more specifically Your Thoughts) to begin to create your life based on your newly found knowledge and begin producing desired results. Just as you would plant the apple seed and receive an apple tree, whatever thought seeds that you release into the Universe must bring back to you in physical form, exactly what you planted.

No more than you would expect a crabgrass seed to produce an Oak tree, can anyone expect the seed thoughts which create doubt, fear, lack, and limitation to produce a harvest of abundance and happiness in your life.

By the same token, if you choose to plant thought seeds which project and create Love, Joy, Peace, Fulfilment, Contentment, Prosperity, etc. you will experience (reap) the harvest of your seeds that harmonise with the original seeds planted. As in the examples above, these same principles are what determine your health and wellness. If your thoughts are constantly focused on health and wellness in your body, you will reap a harvest of health and wellness. If you are constantly focused on sickness and disease or a Fear of such, the Universe will return to you exactly what it is you asked it for, a body full of sickness and disease. It doesn't matter what the situation or circumstance, whether it be health, finances, relationships, etc. The power of thoughts is every bit as creative in health situations as it is with money matters. The power of thoughts... more specifically the power of your thoughts combined with the emotional response that you choose as a result of these thoughts are equally as creative and powerful in your personal relationships as they are in any other part of your life.

Your control over the power of thoughts can only be determined by your willingness to accept the fact that it's true and become consciously aware of the thoughts you choose to think. The bottom line behind all this explaining is...

Change your thoughts, and you Will change your world! Make a conscious and consistent effort, and you will develop the ability to focus the power of thoughts on creating a life far in excess of you may have previously "conceived" or believed was possible for you.

Universal Principles are, always have been and always will be set and fixed. There is no wavering in their perfect and precise operation. You cannot outsmart them, hide from them, or overcome them. They are precise and exact and have existed since the beginning of time itself and will continue to exist and produce in their precise manner into infinity.

They are not prejudice in their implementation. It doesn't matter what your spiritual or religious beliefs are, what gender you are, what your age is or what country you come from. They don't differentiate among people that we perceive as good or bad. They are exact and non-prejudice in delivering to all, exactly the same, in accordance with the seeds that are planted.

Your knowledge of them or ignorance to them is of no consequence. They will continue to be regardless of your awareness or unawareness of them. A person's belief or dis-belief in their power has no effect on their operation. They will continue to operate exactly as they have since the beginning of time whether you believe in them or not.

Once introduced to or made aware of these principles, you have the Power of Choice to do with them what you will. As modern day science has discovered and validated, and spiritual teachers have attempted to teach for thousands of years, our Universe gives back to us exactly what we ask of it through our predominant thought processes. We choose those thought processes...we choose the emotions that we experience and. we choose whatever events, conditions and circumstances that we create in our lives.

We always are receiving an abundance of something. That's how the Universe creates. When you become "conscious" and choose to recognise the creative power of thoughts, you have the potential as well as the ability to transform your entire world.

Are you beginning to understand and really grasping the incredible power of thoughts?

Now that you have a basic understanding of what these principles are, and how the power of thoughts work as they do, let's get in to really the good stuff of how to put these principles to work in your personal life to create the kind and quality of abundance and happiness that you desire. Whether you are "conscious" of it or not, you think an average of 60,000 thoughts per day. Isn't that amazing? The human mind thinks an average of 42 thoughts per minute. I think you'll agree, that is a lot of thinking. Now, let's take a look at what happens to all of these thoughts. This will give you a clear picture of the power of thoughts and their creative ability.

The thoughts that you think about the most (your predominant thoughts) are drawn from "pure consciousness", processed by your conscious mind which then create an electro chemical reaction in the brain. These reactions (vibrations) open Neuro-pathways for the vibrations to travel through the brain. As they travel, they are activating additional brain cells which create an intensified electrochemical reaction or vibration. When the thought (vibration) is repeated the brain then attaches an emotion to it which further intensifies the vibration and even more brain cells are attracted to it. This intensified vibration is then sent to and absorbed into in an incredibly sophisticated part of you that is known as the subconscious mind which stores and immediately begins to act upon the information received.

This part of you (subconscious mind) doesn't differentiate between right and wrong, true or false, good or bad, etc. It only acts as a storage device and stores precisely what is given to it. Based on the information given to it (frequency vibrations) it then goes to work to match those vibrations, based on their frequency and join with, or are attracted by vibrations of an equal frequency in the spiritual realm. This is what creates and shapes your world or reality. This is how the process creates. This is why it is so important to become conscious of and clearly understand the power of thoughts and become consciously aware of what your thoughts are attracting into your world.

Just as the thought vibration (spiritual) began and created a physical reaction in your brain, so the resulting vibrations intensified by an emotion, will seek out and attract like or harmonious vibrations which vibrate at the same frequency, resulting in creation or a physical reaction in your external world. The sad thing is this. Most people go from day to day throughout their lives not only totally unaware of the power of thoughts in producing the lives they desire, but what is equally as sad, is the fact that they aren't consciously aware of exactly what it is they are thinking! they are leaving to chance what they are producing (harvest) through their thinking! Since it's true that your predominant thoughts (seeds) are creative and bring back to you exactly what you ask,(harvest) would it not make good sense to become consciously aware of what these thoughts are, so that you are able to focus them on creating the kind of life that you desire and deserve?

Are you ready to put the power of thoughts to work for you?

Great! that brings us to lesson 1 of how to begin to implement all of these things discussed, into your personal life. This one step can have an immediate and drastic impact on whatever it is you have a desire to accomplish. I can assure you with absolute 100% certainty that internalising and putting into focused and intentional action what you are discovering concerning the power of thoughts will enable and empower you to become a conscious and purposeful creator of the events, conditions and circumstances that make up your life and will yield far more desirable results than remaining an "Unconscious Creator!!

"Become Consciously aware of what you're thinking about, and Change the focus of those thoughts to what you desire to Create for your life"

Sounds simple doesn't it? Don't let the simplicity of this principle fool you. It is extremely powerful! The really good news is that you do have control over your thoughts. Your thoughts, once you learn to become consciously aware of them, do not have control over you. You are in total and complete control of them. Your thoughts do not think you, you think your thoughts. Realising this, it is imperative that you make an effort to become keenly and consciously aware of the quality of thought that you're choosing, if you are to begin to "consciously control" what programming your subconscious mind receives, and begin to have control over what you attract and experience in your life.

Ways to Change your subconscious thoughts

Through my own research and personal experiences concerning the power of thoughts, specifically overwriting subconscious thoughts, it is only necessary to overwrite and replace the undesirable, counterproductive subconscious programming (false beliefs) with information that is congruent with desired outcomes.

Subconscious processes can be changed.

It begins with a conscious choice to enhance and/or elevate the quality of belief quite simply. For some, this is an easy and almost effortless process, for others it can require a bit more discipline. For still others it can prove to be the hardest thing you've ever done. Yet the rewards far outweigh the cost as those who choose that path will openly and happily tell you, myself included. The subconscious mind is immensely more powerful than the conscious mind. In fact some scientists claim that the subconscious is as much as a million times more powerful and in the vast majority of cases it can take commitment. it may require some discipline and initial effort on your part to overwrite and replace the subconscious thought processes which many times you aren't even consciously aware of. I've personally found that an enhanced "intellectual" understanding of the knowledge combined with an "experiential approach" is most effective in shifting and developing the ability to begin consciously utilising the power of thoughts individually. Think of it as a whole brain approach that appeals to both the left brain (intellectual) and right brain (intuitive) aspects of mind.

3

Develop a Positive Self-esteem

The Power of Positive Self-esteem like all power principles is a vitally important principle to understand. A principle that if embraced and applied will enable and empower you to experience the joy, harmony and fulfilment that is readily available to each of us without exception.

In fact a high level of self-esteem is one of the most vital principles for being, doing and having more. It's the foundation that all of your individually chosen thoughts, beliefs, emotions and actions are built upon with regard to ourselves, how we respond and react to others and what we perceive as we encounter various events, conditions and circumstances in life. And each of these chosen ways of "being" also determine...without fail... the kind and quality of our experiences individually in life. Our level of self-esteem impacts and quite literally determines the quality of every aspect of our lives whether physically, financially, relationally, emotionally and spiritually.

According to a broad range of experts, conservatively 85% of people in the world needlessly suffer from a diminished self-esteem. Once you grasp and clearly understand that everything in life is derived from and based on your individually chosen quality of consciousness, it becomes quite apparent that a high level of self-esteem is without question a critical component that's necessary...essential in fact for consciously and consistently attracting and experiencing abundance and happiness which is made real and possible when the physical, financial, relational, emotional and spiritual aspects of life become harmonious.

In other words a high level of self-esteem equates to attracting and experiencing harmonious and fuelling rewarding relationships, material abundance and vibrant and radiant health.

High levels of self-esteem equate to peace of mind, harmony and fulfilment in life. Yet as important as it is...as vital as it is in us "getting what we want", many are "unaware" of its importance and even more importantly how to make the shift should they discover that their individual level of self-esteem conflicts with what they "truly desire" to be, do and/or have in the various areas of their lives.

And that's one of the major reasons...perhaps even the one reason that so many "perceive" that they can't get what they want.

They simply don't possess....based on what they've learned to be true...the level of self-esteem that will enable them to get it.

But it's a self-created dichotomy. And I think it's important to emphasise that it is without exception Self-Created or at the very least self-allowed.

Here's what I mean by that...

The more "correct statement" would be that at some point in our lives we've "allowed it" to happen as we were growing up, and in that situation, it's not our fault for sure. In fact it's vital that we do not allow ourselves to get into the place that we "perceive" it to be anyone's fault...regardless .Not ours...not those who taught us...not anyone. Because in the bigger scheme of things, it's not anyone's fault in the literal sense of the word. In the vast majority of cases everyone does the best they can as they teach us what they believe to be "true and real and right" about life based on where they are in their understanding.

It's vital that we accept that and learn to understand it...internalise it and most importantly live by it. It's a chosen way of being that will enable us to reclaim our power and be that much closer to consciously, intentionally and consistently mastering the ability to begin "getting what we want."

And we do, without exception each have the very same ability to do so. It's simply a matter of choice. Because regardless of what it is we've been taught and accepted as being true, it's just "data"...externally acquired data that we've learnt and accepted as being "true." Attempting to find fault or blame in ourselves or others whether it be past, present or future, only serves to keep us from moving towards what we want.

In fact, it keeps us stuck in undesirable cycles...

- ...For others
- ...For ourselves
- ...For our "perceived failures"
- ...For our mistakes
- ...For our shortcomings
- ...For all of it

Choosing to adopt this "way of being" empowers ourselves, enables us to break through the "perceived barriers" that we "believe" are so real and enables us to move forward. Yet in far too many cases we've allowed the beliefs, perceptions and opinions of others to dictate, determine and in a number of cases undermine what we all innately "know" to be true about ourselves, our capabilities and the infinite possibilities that are equally available to each of us.

whether you currently understand it or not...whether you choose to believe or not believe it currently...below all the layers of "beliefs and perceptions" that we've allowed ourselves to acquire throughout life...we each "know" at the deepest place within ourselves just how "true" it is.

We just have to remove the layers to "remember." and choosing to do so, consciously and intentionally restores and elevates our individual self-esteem. In the bigger scheme of things it's these layers...unfounded beliefs and perceptions that we choose, which blind us to the awesomeness, uniqueness and greatness that we "truly are."

We become conditioned and indoctrinated to "forget" that we were each created in the "Image and likeness of Source, whatever you might perceive Source to be.

Through what we've learnt to be real, right and true about ourselves, about life, about what we can have and not have, we perceive....whether at a conscious or subconscious level that we are in some way, shape or form flawed..."unworthy" of receiving the heartfelt desires we all have which in turn makes us incapable of making them real.

How and Why do we do that? The how is by allowing the beliefs, perceptions and opinions of others to affect, mould and shape what we believe and how we think about ourselves. It really is as simple as that.

*Consider this...*In the vast majority of cases we're not even "consciously aware" of why we believe what we believe. In the vast majority of cases you can ask someone "why" they believe what they believe and the answer is "Because it's true."

But in far more cases than not it's only "perceived" as being "true" due to being indoctrinated with the perceptions and beliefs of others without ever taking the time or the initiative to discover if these acquired "beliefs and perceptions" are "really true."

Although granted our "belief in them" has made them "real and true" in the various areas of our lives and the outcomes experienced thus far solidify our "beliefs and perceptions" as to how "true" they are.

Yet, it doesn't make it "Really true"...it's only our beliefs and perceptions, as limited and self-sabotaging as they might be, which have created and will continue creating outcomes that always harmonise with our choices.

As true as we might "perceive" them...as real as they might seem based on our "beliefs" and the experiences these "beliefs have created at some point in the past...regardless of how much we love and trust those who have taught us what is "real, right and true" in the various areas of our lives, there exists a "Higher Truth." There is always a "Higher Truth."

There is no "limit" to truth. Truth...our "chosen truth" is infinite in nature and only delivers to us in life just as we choose for it to. To experience greater outcomes, it's necessary to make some different choices. And the greatest choice we can make is choosing to elevate our belief in ourselves which in turn elevates the level of self-esteem that we are choosing and have chosen for ourselves.

When we "choose" to do that we can begin removing all the layers and we begin "getting more of what we want."

And I can assure you based on personal experience and assisting countless others globally to get to the core of why they believe what they believe, in Far More cases than not what so many "believe and perceive" as being "true" about themselves and their capabilities isn't true at all.

They've simply been "taught" that it's true, and as a result "believe it." They've never questioned and as a result never explored beyond the "externally acquired data" that they've been exposed to and chosen to adopt and live by as "their truth."

Due to these "chosen beliefs", we act out in life through our individually chosen thoughts, words and deeds based on what we "believe and perceive" as being true regarding life and ourselves and the immutable, unwavering perfection of the creative process harmonizes with our choice and we "experience" a kind and quality of life just as we choose.

We've "chosen" to accept the "beliefs" that we're imperfect, flawed and limited. It's us who has "accepted the fact" that we're born into sin and unworthy. And due to those choices, we become and experience just that based on those chosen beliefs.

Through various means, we're indoctrinated beginning in the earliest years of childhood to "believe" that we're unworthy...not good enough...in some way flawed. We're taught and have developed "beliefs" that getting what we want is "hard", not possible, requires struggle and that "the chips just fall as they will." And we always get to be right. We always get to experience life just as we choose.

Although this indoctrination can and often does happen in the most innocent of ways and with the best of intentions, it's done nonetheless. And we have allowed it.

We're not taught about how awesome and powerful and creative we are. We're not "taught" about the inalienable gifts we've been provided to create or if you prefer co-create our lives consciously and intentionally in a way that we "truly desire."

We're taught and "believe" how limited we are. We're "taught" what's rational, logical, practical and "doable or not doable" for ourselves. As a result, we create and experience our lives in a way that harmonizes with what we've chosen. As a result of not understanding why we believe what we believe we go through life "unconsciously creating" and fail to see how our individual power...what we "know and believe" to be true is creating whatever is happening around us just as we choose.

Unless and until we make a "conscious and intentional choice" to discover otherwise, unless and until we choose to accept responsibility for our lives and consciously choose to elevate the quality of what we've come to "believe" and "know" to be true about our lives...our "true capabilities...and the infinite nature of what's "truly available" to and for each of us, this indoctrination can and often does impact and affect our results for our entire lives.

We unnecessarily and unknowingly remain limited by our own choices. And just as we choose...life delivers it to us...Without fail and with unwavering certainty. So it's vital first of all that we accept responsibility for our lives and our outcomes.

We don't "have to" but we can "choose to" whenever we "decide to." Although many never venture outside of their chosen beliefs...although they'll choose to look outside of themselves for why and how things in life turn out as they do...it's nothing more than a choice to remain limited by what others have told and taught them about themselves.

And for those who choose to remain stuck in that mind-set...those who choose to hold that "quality of belief" it impacts and determines the entire course of their lives regardless of how "desirable or undesirable" that quality of life might be.

But it's nothing more than a choice. An individual and in the vast majority of cases an "unconscious choice" but a choice nonetheless. The why we "allow" that to happen is simply because we all, at the deepest levels of ourselves have a desire to be loved, appreciated and accepted. We want to fit in. That is at the core of why we do whatever we do, why we act the way we act which inevitably results in what we have or don't have.

Granted, sometimes it doesn't "seem" that way when we observe others "doing so" in way that hurts or somehow adversely affects others. It's difficult to "see" how we ourselves do so when we're coming from a place of fear, lashing out and reacting adversely....but underlying every choice we make and everything that we do, we do for that reason and that reason only. We simply want to be loved, accepted and appreciated.

And we each do that based on what we "believe and perceive" as being true. The infinite number of ways that we express that innate desire outwardly in our attempts to get what we all want as individuals is done in the way it is based on our individually held "perceptions and beliefs" with regard to what's necessary for us to do so.

But this "fitting in"...this desire to be loved, appreciated and accepted by "buying into" and living by what the "vast majority" believes and "perceives" as being the right and only way, limits our abilities to be, do and have what we "truly desire." We adopt the mind-set of the vast majority. We develop a "steeple people" mentality. We believe as the vast majority does and as a result experience a quality of life that the vast majority always will.

I can assure you that the vast majority has a very limited perspective regarding their "True Power" and as a result choose a very limiting level of self-esteem for themselves.

To rise above the limitation...to experience a "greater quality of life", it's vital that we adopt a "Higher Truth" than the vast majority chooses to. It's vital that we discover that our lives,...the kind and quality of our lives is only limited by what we are and have been choosing for ourselves which precipitates an "Awakening."

The greatest realisation we can come to is with regards to ourselves. The power that we've each been equally provided to create a kind and quality of life limited only by our individual choices. And once we see that..."once we choose" to recognise and awaken to our "true power", our self-esteem...what we know to be true about ourselves is elevated and our world harmonises with that choice. We begin to "see and experience" a shift in the world around us. We begin getting "more of what we want."

How is it that a sense of high esteem of self is so important in achieving harmony, fulfilment, abundance and happiness in life?

It's quite logical and very simple to comprehend once you're "aware of" and choose to understand how the Universal Laws that govern the entire cosmos operate. Once you've become "aware of" and choose to develop a deeper understanding of the law Of Vibration and have a basic understanding of the fact that all things, both the seen as well as the unseen, broken down and analysed in their purest form consist of pure energy (E=MC2)...that all energy consists of and vibrates at a certain vibratory frequency the quality of which determines quality .

Once you have developed a basic understanding of how these energies attract to you the events conditions, and circumstances that happen in your day to day life due to the immutable, unwavering and unerring nature of the Law Of attraction based on the resonance of that energy, you will have developed a crystal clear understanding of the importance of developing a sense of positive self-esteem.

And the bottom line is our beliefs regarding ourselves, what is possible or not possible for ourselves, is what determines this "projected frequency."

Let's look at it from a strictly "scientific perspective"...

Your "chosen way of being" emits and projects a resonance...a projected frequency of energy that without fail is projected into what 21st century science refers to as "the field." This "field" is what scientists refer to as an "infinite field" where all probabilities already exist.

Our individual choices...our chosen beliefs regarding ourselves creates and projects a frequency into this "field" transmuting the infinite waves of probability existing in the field from waves of probability into particles of matter. What you experience in the various areas of your life...the events, conditions, circumstances always provides a mirrored reflection of that choice or choices.

The quality of the frequency is determined by the quality of the belief or beliefs that you choose for yourself.

Let's examine specifically how these two perceived conflicting states...these "chosen states"...both high self-esteem and low self-esteem attract and create the results that they do.

First we'll look at positive or high self-esteem.....

Positive self-esteem could be looked at as a "higher vibrational intensity" of energy and a low sense of self-esteem representing a lower vibrational intensity.

Positive self-esteem projects and expresses your love of self...a higher form of energy frequency and therefore projects this "higher frequency" into "the field" allowing you to attract "higher energies" that harmonise with your choice.

 Positive self-esteem is experienced when you fully grasp and understand who and what you "truly are" your worth in the bigger scheme of things and clearly understand that regardless of the inevitable mistakes that we all make during life, regardless of the "perceived failures" we may encounter and experience as we learn and grow, they are nothing more or less than stepping stones that...should we "allow" them to...lead you to the "desired outcome."

Positive self-esteem is being able to laugh at yourself, learn from yourself, honour and love yourself. Positive self-esteem is achieved through mastering the ability based on an unconditional love of self, absent judgments.

Being in this state of Positive self-esteem creates a specific vibratory frequency which is broadcast into the Universe and through the Law of Attraction attracts to you energies of the same vibratory frequency which through a process of time manifest in physical form based on those positive frequencies.

Low Self Esteem

Low self-esteem is based on judgment of yourself. Low self-esteem of self happens due to the fact that those that choose it hold on to internal judgments of some form and in which they feel inferior or less than whole.

Many times these feelings of unworthiness are established based on childhood experiences. Just as with positive self-esteem, a sense of low self-esteem also vibrates at a specific frequency, varying in intensity than that of positive self-esteem (a much lower frequency) which attracts to you additional energies that harmonise with the outgoing frequency and creates outcomes or life experiences based on the kind and quality of those frequencies.

When you choose to remain stuck in a state of low self-esteem or unworthiness, you are in reality communicating to the Universe that you don't deserve all that it has to provide you...which is Infinite in nature and therefore attract and create a reality that harmonises with your choice in each and every area of your life.

Low self-esteem comes about as a result of feeling a sense of separateness. It is important to understand that you are not separate from the Whole but instead an integral part of the Whole. Regardless of individual human perception the Whole is perfect. The Whole is and consists of Unconditional Love absent any judgment whatsoever. This includes judgment of self. Judgment, whether that of self or that of others is contrary to and conflicts with the unchangeable Universal Ideal of Unconditional Love.

A state of low self-esteem can be likened to that of resistance. In a state of resistance you emanate and project a specific vibratory energy which can only attract more of that which you resist.

It is extremely important to understand that regardless of your preconceived perceptions, you are absolutely perfect just the way you are. Once you have developed the ability to recognise this "Higher Truth", and begin eliminating self-judgment as well as judgment of those around you, you will have come to a place that opens the door of unlimited blessings, profound inner peace, and a sense of overall well-being.

Your perceptions of self and everything in our universe are based only on your beliefs; many times previously established false beliefs. A common false belief among those who have a low sense of self-esteem is that they are not worthy of receiving all that they are entitled to. It is due to these same false beliefs and perceptions that make you feel inferior which draws to you events, conditions and circumstances that harmonise with your choice. Outcomes that are "inferior" to what you "truly want."

Your perceptions and beliefs of truth with regard to yourself do not make it truth; it only becomes your truth, and therefore becomes your reality. In the same way, others "perceptions and beliefs" regarding you don't make it true and have no impact on you unless and until you choose to allow them to. The fact that you believe it is true initiates the Law of attraction to bring to you in physical form precisely that which you believe to be true. If you feel unworthy, the Universe can only deliver to you results in alignment with what and how you feel and believe to be true.

In reality you are not inferior at all, but it is only your belief that makes it so. Your reality is brought about and made physical by those things that you have come to believe are true. Low self-esteem and feelings of inferiority are based on beliefs that you are not worthy of those things that have been promised to you.

Look around you and think about the infinite number of things that currently exist all around you. Which of those things do you most desire? They too, whatever they may be are also a part of the whole, of the Universe, of existence. Are you, also being an integral and important part of the whole, not also worthy of receiving them? The answer...your individual answers...whether it be Yes or No will determine what you have or don't have. Whatever you believe to be so.

Your beliefs and perceptions whether based on a sense of inferiority or an understanding of your worthiness attract and bring to you more of whichever you choose in exact proportion to that which you feel you deserve. (or don't deserve).

In a state of positive self-esteem you are in a state that projects to the Universe that you are worthy of all that it holds for you and the result is that those things, whatever they might be, are attracted to you and are only limited by what you can conceive and believe to be reality. Shed the false and self-limiting beliefs that you hold concerning your self-worth and you will begin to experience the power of unconditional love of self and in turn for all of humanity.

You are perfect in every way exactly as you are. Your perception and belief that you are somehow broken, or inferior, implies that you are not receiving all that has been made available to you, and will limit those things that can be attracted and given to you. Once you have come to this understanding and begin to take correct action on what you have discovered, you will have opened a channel of communication and blessings which will guide you and allow you to attract and experience those things that you most desire. You will have discovered the key to living and experiencing a life uncommon to so many.

So, how do you begin to accomplish this? What specific steps are necessary to establish your true sense of worth and come to understand that you are an important, integral and significant part of the whole?

* Go within

* Conceive

* Visualise

* Desire

* Believe

* Achieve

* Experience

And it (whatever it may be) will manifest itself into physical reality. You cannot change the process of creation, but you can change your beliefs and perceptions as to what will be created and experienced as reality in your world. Your outcomes in life are based only on your beliefs as to what is possible and those beliefs, more specifically what those beliefs are empowered to attract, are limited only by your self-esteem and what you feel that you are worthy (or not worthy) of receiving.

The possibilities available to you are infinite in nature. The qualities of those possibilities are limited only by the choices that you make for yourself.

You truly are a creator of if you prefer a co-creator of your reality. Develop your understanding of this immutable and unwavering truth...this "Higher Truth" and come to the realisation that you are perfect in every way just the way you are, and that which you are enabled to attract and experience will far exceed anything that you have previously experienced.

You, I and everyone else have been provided this incredible and irrevocable gift by the Source of creation; whatever you might "perceive" this Source to be. Discover your importance in the process. Develop the understanding that you are a very important and integral part of the Whole and you will have come to a place of Unconditional Self Love which will turn your life into an incredible journey of joy, fulfilment, profound inner peace, and unlimited blessings in each and every area of your life. Your individual consciousness is a part of Universal Consciousness. Likewise Universal Consciousness Is Part of your consciousness. You are a very important, necessary and integral part of Universal Consciousness. (The Whole) Absent your individual consciousness the whole would not be whole but only a part. Nothing can be whole without all the parts. You are a very real and important part that makes up the whole. Without you "The Whole" is only a part and not whole.

Regardless of your current perception and belief, or perceived separation, you cannot be truly separated from the whole, for that is reality. It is only through your beliefs and perceptions that can and do separate you from that reality and the result is that you feel separate. The Whole cannot and will not separate from you, but through free will you have been given the choice to separate from it. This choice is made real by those things that you believe to be true. If you don't feel that you are a part of the whole, it is that very feeling, that belief that will separate you from it. The result of this perceived separateness is experienced in fear, anxiety and a sense of aloneness. The result of these perceived experiences is, through the Law of attraction (Unconditional Love) attracting more of that which you fear and are anxious about.

You are never truly shut off from the whole. It is only your false beliefs or a misguided perception that makes it appear to be so. You have the ability to open the door any time you choose to do so. You also have the choice to close that same door at your choosing. The door will only open as wide as you are able to conceive and believe that it can.

The whole is always present and waiting for you to except it's truth, it's reality. What is that reality? That you are an incredible and magnificent creature created in the image and likeness of your creator and have been provided the means in which to create that which is limited only by your ability to believe it so. That is the real truth. When you utilise your free will to believe in those things which are false and perceive those things which are contrary to Unconditional Love, the Universe through its fixed, unwavering, omnipresent, omniscient Unconditional Love, provides to you exactly that which you have asked for based on that belief.

Discover your true worth, learn to experience Unconditional Love of self and realise that anything and everything that you have done in the past or will do in the future has a specific and definitive purpose that, regardless of your current belief or perception, will benefit the whole.

Change your beliefs as well as your perceptions as to those things that you experience in your life Understand that when you become fearful concerning a circumstance that you are experiencing, it will persist and continue until you have learnt the lesson that it was intended to teach you. Once you have passed that test life will inevitably lead you to the next.

Your positive self-esteem combined with a deeper understanding that all things work together for the good of the Whole will change your perceptions and beliefs concerning those events and therefore change those experiences that you come to know and experience as your reality. Acceptance of these truths will allow your life journey to become an exciting and anticipated series of events, eager to move on to the next lesson and a higher plane of understanding.

Belief to Perception to thought to Vibration to Emotion to Attraction to External Reality.

Your positive self-esteem can and will allow that external reality to become as great as you can conceive it to be. Likewise a sense of low self-esteem can and will only allow your external reality to become as great as you can conceive it and believe it to be.

Do you feel worthy? You are. You only have to discover the real truth concerning that worth.

You have been provided the ability to choose how you feel. You have been provided the ability to change those beliefs that conflict with the highertruth concerning who and what you are and your undeniable worth in our universe. You have also been provided the free will to experience your life any way you choose.

4

How to attract abundance and Success

You know in today's busy, high stress and hustle bustle world, it's become rather obvious that the vast majority are attempting to create abundance in the various areas of their lives through any number of external venues and in the process often overlook a far more rewarding and fulfilling way to do so.

Another thing that's become very obvious is that this predominantly chosen way of "doing things" isn't yielding the kind, quality or quantity of results that so many consistently hope and wish and pray" that it would.

Have you ever considered the idea of "attracting abundance" rather than chasing and working and "trying" so hard to get it? No...it doesn't eliminate action by any means but it most certainly produces far greater results with far less "displeasing effort."

So how do you begin doing this attracting abundance thing?

Well, it begins by making some slight shifts in the way you've been "doing things." This shift equates mainly to choosing an inside- out approach to life rather than the way most choose which is strictly based on an outside approach. The Inside Out approach begins by making a conscious and intentional choice to elevate your level of awareness.

Attracting abundance, happiness and "Real Success" into your life is only dependent on and determined by your level of awareness.

Although external forms of wealth are most certainly a sought after and "desirable" experience for most, what's most often overlooked is the fact that the acquisition of these externals whether of a physical, financial, relational, emotional or spiritual nature are much more simple to acquire and experience than the vast majority "perceive."

That's why those who achieve uncommon results in life are such a small minority. They understand and choose to do what the vast majority don't.

Yet this "Doing" doesn't begin and end with "physical activity" as the vast majority "perceive."Experiencing an Uncommon Kind and Quality of Life For yourself requires nothing more and nothing less than "Consciously Choosing" an Inside Out approach to Life.

What does that mean exactly? Quite simply, it means that choosing to align and harmonise the internal aspects of you with whatever form of success and wealth you desire for yourself first, enables the externals to become much more simple to acquire.

In fact, you begin to "attract them." That's why so many strive and "try so hard" to acquire with such limited results. They simply choose to overlook and bypass this first essential step.

By first developing a keen awareness of self and the power provided to you to be, do and have whatever you choose and then consistently applying the success principles that make it all possible, you can, regardless of any pre-established notions you may have held regarding your ability to do so, attain a level of harmony and fulfilment in life that few perceive to have the time to develop and as a result never take the time to discover the ease and simplicity of opening "The Flow" of abundance that doing so can provide.

Yet ironically at the same time it's this choice that would enable them to fully grasp and understand where their "true power" lies and provide far more of what they truly want in far greater quantity than their current choices could ever hope to provide.

This understanding combined with a willingness to consciously harmonise your thought, word, deed and "consciously held intention" with these principles, initiates a force so powerful that no currently "perceived" obstacle can keep you from achieving whatever level of abundance, happiness and success that you can conceive and envision for yourself. By discovering, understanding, and "consciously" implementing the following success principles, the kind and quality of life you'll become enabled and empowered to experience can and will be limited only by the restrictions that you place upon yourself.

The Power to take a bold step: What makes successful people reach their goals in life? Here's a simple answer for you. They decide that they want to get rich. They decide that they need to do something about their desire. They decide on what, when and how to do their lifetime plan for success.

The power of decision is very crucial in success. Once you decided what your plans are and how to do it, then action would soon follow. But without making a decision, then you have nothing to work on, would you? If you have this one great idea on how you can make your own wealth base, then never sit on it. You should decide when and how you could put your ideas into concrete actions. Never delay your dreams. Procrastination would eat you up and all your ideas would turn into nothing if you don't decide what to do with it. Time is a very important factor to consider when creating your decision.

How do you come up with a good decision? One basic thing about decision-making is that you should have a definite purpose for it. Be true to yourself and you should know what your true intentions are. By knowing this, then you would be able to make the right decision to accomplish your goals.

A decision should be done with an open-mind. Know what your odds are and create an objective pro and con list. You should have all your options lying down in front of your face before making any decision. Do not be satisfied with choices A and B. What do you know, choices C or D might be the right one for you.

You would never know what a right or wrong decision is unless that decision is put to the test. It is important that you always prepare for the worst and accept failure if it does come your way.

This doesn't mean that you have to be a negative thinker but you should be open to the idea that you can fail. With this kind of thinking, you allow yourself to be ready for the things that might happen if your plan doesn't turn out good. A back-up plan can save dreams.

In case of failure, you should be able to tweak your action plan quite easily. Sometimes an overhaul or drastic change may not be necessary. You should be able to change your decisions with a gradual implementation if there's a need for a change. Most successful people do change their decision a lot of times along the way, but they do so in a timely manner.

Your power of decision should be strong enough to compel you to take actions, not tomorrow or next week, but today. The earlier you decide on what your plans are and how to implement it, the faster you would be in the throne of success. Unleash the Power of your mind and subconscious mind and catapult yourself to Success

Mind power is about more than just positive thinking. Once you realize that it is the power of your thoughts and beliefs that create your reality, you will begin to pay close attention to the thoughts you are thinking. By working with the process in the e-course and audio program you will learn how to direct the power of your mind and subconscious mind to create the life you want.

Developing your Subconscious Mind Power is a straightforward, effective process based on the power of thoughts and the power of your subconscious mind.

When you work with your subconscious Mind Power you learn how to use affirmations, visualisation, and the many other techniques that will aid you in harnessing the power of your subconscious mind. It goes beyond simple positive thinking and gives you a system that you can apply everyday so that you regularly direct your subconscious mind to create the positive and rewarding life you want.

Once you master your Mind Power and unleash your subconscious mind power, will help you develop the personal power that you already possess to create success and fulfilment in life. Positive, daily affirmations will help and will show you how to get the most out of them as well as how to develop powerful visualisation process that will lead to greater success in every area of your life.

5

Putting skills acquired to use

Adopt, Adapt, Improve and Innovate

Adapting ideas that have worked in one environment and using them in another is one of the most successful of innovation techniques.

In 1916, a young American scientist and inventor called Clarence Birdseye went to Canada as a fur trader. He noticed that people in Labrador kept their food frozen in the snow for extended periods in the winter. When he returned to the U.S. he developed this idea and launched a line of quick-frozen foods and persuaded retailers to stock them in freezers. He created the frozen food industry. Birdseye subsequently sold his business to General Foods Corporation and made his fortune.

Alexander Graham Bell studied the workings of the human ear. He adapted the idea of the eardrum vibrating with sounds into the workings of a metal diaphragm which led to his invention of the telephone.

The motto of the round table is adopt, adapt, improve and it is an excellent guideline for implementing new ideas in your business. Taking ideas from other environments and adapting them for use in your situation is one of the best ways of implementing novel solutions. Amar Bhide of the Harvard Business School studied the origin and evolution of new businesses. He found that over 70% of successful start-ups were based on ideas that the founders had adopted from their previous employments. They took a promising idea in a field they understood and made it better.

The person who invented the roll-on deodorant was looking for a new way to apply a liquid. He copied an idea from another field, writing, where the same problem is solved.

Samuel Morse was the inventor of morse code. He encountered a problem sending signals over long distances on the telegraph - the signal became attenuated and weak. Then one day when he was travelling by stagecoach he noticed how the coach changed horses at relay stations. He adapted this idea to put in relay stations for telegraphs.

In 1941 George de Mestral went for a walk with his dog in the Jura mountains in Switzerland. On their return he noticed that many plant burrs were attached to his trousers and to the dog's coat. They were hard to remove. He examined them under the microscope and saw that they contained tiny hooks that caught in the loops of his clothes and in the dog's hair. He developed an artificial material to mimic nature.

If you have a problem try to force fit a link with a random event or animal or institution. Then adapt some ideas from that environment. Say your problem is how to motivate a lethargic team and you choose at random the Olympic Games, a tiger and a Ballet school. What sorts of ideas would that trigger? You might offer medals as recognition for top performers. You could keep records of who has achieved the fastest qualified lead or the fastest assembly time and post them on the wall or the extranet in the form of Olympic records. The tiger might suggest face painting as a trick for raising morale or it might suggest hunting - you could have a treasure hunt in the office or organise a 'hunt for sales' competition. And so on. The ballet school students practice all their exercises each day before they perform a dance. This might suggest a high-energy group practice session each morning before work proper begins. Ballet dancers practice in front of mirrors - what if we installed systems that gave us feedback to build the team's motivation?

Alternatively, try to adapt a combination between your organisation's main strength and that of other organisations or people. Say you provide high level training courses and you choose at random a hospital then you might come up with the idea of a consulting accident and emergency clinic where people turn up with their problems and you help diagnose them on the spot. Or you may ponder that many people forget what they learn on training courses. In a hospital patients have on-going physiotherapy sessions to aid recovery. This idea could be adapted so that you send out "physio trainers" to top up the learning of participants after they have completed their courses. Alternatively, if you think of the

Boy Scouts then you might imagine a summer camp for some of your top clients or a "bob a job" campaign where you offer short introductory courses for new clients.

Lateral thinking is about finding new ways to solve problems. It is very likely that the current problem you face at work today has been faced and solved by other people. Maybe they were in your line of business or maybe they confronted a similar problem but in an entirely different walk of life. Why do all the brain work yourself when you can adapt someone else's idea and make it work for you?

Tips for finding ideas you can adopt and adapt:

. Take time out to discuss your problem with people from entirely different backgrounds. If you are a businessman then ask a teacher or a priest or a musician.

.Read a different magazine, visit a different environment, see a foreign movie, drive a new route home, find some new inspiration in a different source.

. Place yourself in a different environment and it will help you see concepts and ideas you can adapt. If you visit an Eskimo in his igloo, like Clarence Birdseye, you may come back with an idea as good as the one that built the frozen food industry.

. Identify analogous situations in other fields and ask how they would be handled.

If you are able to put all that you have read into use, you are on the pathway to Success.